Dear Dawn
and Daylight

Dear Dawn and Daylight

Ndaba Sibanda

Clara Songbirds
Publishing House

Clare Songbirds Publishing House Poetry Series
ISBN 978-1-957221-30-4
Clare Songbirds Publishing House
Dear Dawn and Daylight © 2025 Ndaba Sibanda

Printed in the United States of America
FIRST EDITION

140 Cottage Street
Auburn, New York 13021
www.claresongbirdspub.com

Heads up a little…
What did Africa contribute to the world?
Humanity—of course, and heavenly sites.

Acknowledgements:

The author wishes to thank the following publishers for originally publishing the poems in this work:

"Dawn" in *Whispers*, March 2013
"Esigodini Hills" in *Outside In Literary & Travel Magazine*, June 2014
"Esigodini Hills" in *Metaphor Magazine*, February 2014
"Of Condom and Sodom" in *Piker Press*, December 2013
"Of Condom and Sodom" in *Poetrypotion.com*, July 2013

Contents

Haven't A Million   1

Of Condom And Sodom   2

From Scars To Stars   3

Hello Beautiful Nami   4

The Eyes Of A Visitor   5

Get Up And Find It   6

Sunlight   7

Dawn   9

I Can`t Get Enough Of It   10

Falling Into The Falls   12

The Explorer And The Claimant   14

The Hotel Music   16

Isitshwala   17

Mopani Worms   18

A Done Deal   19

Esigodini Hills   20

Romance Tourism   22

Voices In The Caves   23

Haven't A Million

Yes, my pen
Is in my den
It is my spear
I shall not fear

They go to the fields
My words my shields

Yes, my pen
Is in my den
It is my spear
I shall not fear

Rich with my words
Mightier than swords

Words apt and raw
I roar a royal roar!

I'm a roaring lion
Haven't a million

I roar a royal roar!
Lion lion lion lion

I roar a royal ROARRR!!

Of Condom And Sodom

Be the catalyst for positive change
Not the beggar for cents and change

Free yourself from violence and drugs
March to financial freedom from the rags

The freedom train is running really fast
On the rails informed by a heroic past

Youth of today don`t be a political condom
Seek no populist refuge in corruption`s Sodom

From Scars To Stars

There has to be development
You owe it to posterity
To strive for your betterment
There has to be prosperity

Didn`t the parents bear the brunt
Of cultural and social and economic
Scars of history in a sublime fashion?

There has to be development
You owe it to posterity
To strive for your betterment
There has to be prosperity

Hello Beautiful Nami

The land that is home to beautiful scenery,
Visiting Namibia is like taking an excursion
To a heaven of deserts and wildlife reserves;
It is like exploring the lovely curves of a lover.
A rich experience that transports and transforms,
And leaves one mesmerised tenfold times ten!
The dynamism of natural sceneries is startling,
Its coast is not costly when it comes to coolness,
There is a celebration of diversity and splendour;
The menu has an African and European flavour,
It is a mixed dish of ethos, cultures and languages
That has seen many a visitor swallow up their tongue!

The Eyes Of A Visitor

An excursion to a ...
Coastal southern African nation.
Eyes feasting on this country`s natural beauty,
Marveling at great rivers, waterfalls and scenic coastline.
Cruising through different climates, landscapes, cultures and colours,
Catching sight of the amazing Valley of the Moon and the Kalandula Waterfalls-
All the way to the Black Stones of Pungo Adongo before taking a rest at the Coatinha Beach,
The jaunt is not over till one visits the Bay of Luanda, Tazua Falls, Big Welwitschia and Luanda Island.

Get Up And Find It

There could be a rumble
Here and there
Because of life`s storms

There could be a fumble
Here and there
Because you are human

There could be a tumble
Hard and hideous
Because of a slip-up

Life rumbling at you
Roar at it with vigour
Right the wrongs

Life frowning at you
Tantrums thrown at you
Laugh loudly at them

Life hard and hideous
Hold on and hack
Off all the dents

It isn`t always light
Yet seek your light
Life will be bright

For life is but a start
Whose star is in you
Get up and find it.

Sunlight

Sunlight, it is right,
you have no choice,
you are in my heart,
you are on the horizon
of the African breasts.

Dawn in Africa created with Midjourney AI

Dawn

Those who dream
and value Time
live to see a Dawn.

But doomed into
the ruins of a Dinosaur
are those that forever
Dilly-Dally.

For theirs is Drowning
and Dropping
Till history judges
them Harshly.

I Can`t Get Enough Of It

Please , please
take me there,
Let me have a blast,
Not once, not the last.

I seek to unwind…
until I can`t be found!
Yes, nowhere else but…
in the heart of the
Matobo National Park!

Fun galore…
Nature`s bliss mollifies
my soul at the Maleme Dam,
No, I want to go wild and jump
Over the giant granite boulders
overlooking the dam.

I have a must-attend meeting with
the gregarious reptiles there too!
Oh on the agenda is fun and fun,
We shall sit on those rocks and
chit-chat. No biting business today!

By the way, I would like to reach
the summit of Malindindzimu,
'the hill of benevolent spirits'
and experience the wonder
Cecil Rhodes called
" View of the World".

The San`s rock paintings
will certainly rock and
roll with me.

I am an ever-hungry consumer of
information, so the interpretive museum
at the Pomongwe Caves will come in handy!

Oh please take me there,
I want to feel home,
I want to feel the majestic African sun
brighten me up. Its rays kiss my face
and forehead with that unique tenderness.

Please accompany me to the Whovi Wild Area
which is home to several bird species
and lots of species of mammals.
Oh what a sight…

Look at the black and white rhinoceros,
the zebra, the giraffe, the antelope, the leopard,
the flat-footed cheetah, the brown hyena.

I am a fan of guided walks and pony.
Of course I will go fishing in some
of the dams in the Matobo National Park
before I disappear into one of those thatched lodges.
I need to slow down, cool down a little. Re-energise.
Tuck into something finger-licking good. Here I know
they serve one with mouth-watering stuff and comfort!

On the following day another paradise
waits for me. The mighty Victoria
Falls! This is Africa, dear. I can`t
get enough of this continent`s
heavenly tourist centres.

Falling Into The Falls

It is a place many a dignitary
Or world star has graced or dreams of
Without a shred of doubt it constitutes
One of the most awesome natural wonders of the world

On the southern bank
Of the Zambezi River
At the western end of the Victoria
Falls themselves is the Victoria Falls town

The Victoria Falls are a cut above the rest
No wonder the local people call that place
"—Mosi-oa-Tunya"
Meaning 'The smoke that thunders"

A World Heritage Site
No matter how unbreakable
His memory invariably breaks
The layers of time

No matter what
He cannot escape
His is an eternal reminiscence
Hers a tantalising presence

Of the whole scenario
Incredible duo stronger than a trio

No matter how far-flung
It may seem or sound
His heart traverses over proximity
From one zone to blissful probity

They came and cherished
Smiles lighting up the zone
Bodies sinking emotions to
A startling depth
Echoing music epitomising
A graceful warmth

Falling...
Falling into Victoria Falls
Falling and falling
With funny falling feelings

He caught sight of something magical about the Falls
The soaring column of shower when the river was high
The roaring rumble of the cascading water—what a thunder
The awe-inspiring gorge and the serene inlets upstream
Hippo and lethal crocodiles which reign in those lagoons

Suddenly before they knew it
Their passions were but
Ragingly white-water rafting
Hearts canoeing to a pounding halt

He marvels at the wonders of nature
He recalls the moment he tamed
Time and world to a standstill marionette
And a mere palm-captive

Or was he the prisoner
And puppet of the moment?
Or did she hold him
And time firmly in her palm?

He also evokes the magic
Of the Matobo Hills
How they strut their stuff
Of historical splendor

Spellbinding scenery
Cornucopia of heritage that
Sweeps one off one's feet

The memories mortalised
Revisit and drown him
Leaving him with a heightened
Desire to rewind the units of time...

The Explorer and the Claimant

She has travelled to many a country,
Bongile is the daughter of a magnate,

Every man would like to get to know
Her better or to call her one's sister,

It is said one admirer used to camp
Outside her state-of –the art house,

They say after his heart was turned down
The vagrant-turned resident also lost his mind,

It is also said her chauffeur was fired—
Not because he was a reckless driver,

The guy claimed they were an iron red -hot item,
He alleged she had a huge fascination for him,

In fact he said, 'She calls me her first and last fiancé,
I call her the precious Princess of My Heart'.

He claimed they had gone through roadblocks of life together,
He was her hero to weather all her storms on earth,

Together they had gone through jungles and deep rivers,
Together they had triumphed over lions and elephants,

Boasting of having roundly explored her cute curves
While discovering the architecture of famous cities,

He spoke of the mystique of deserts and safaris,
He described the compelling game parks in Kenya,

He dwelt on how as inseparable love birds they tracked
Amazing mountain gorillas in Uganda and in other African nations,

How they experienced the haunting splendour
Of the green rainforest in the Great Lakes,

Of paddling canoes in Malawi and Zimbabwe,
Of thrilling encounters with pure wildlife, her kisses,

All these stories circulated and gave birth to many versions,
But the bottom line is that she eventually got wind of them,

'Bongie likes whale watching, while I take pleasure
In skinning alive my whale on the beaches'

The friend in whom he thought he was confiding,
Went straight to Bongile and cleared his throat,

Before saying,' He claims you are a whale
He likes beaching breathlessly!'

The friend who also wanted to garner marks
And attract her attention was happy with his move,

For Bongile rushed to her personal driver, and yelled,
"You little punk, you `re bush-walking with lies! You`re fired!"

The Hotel Music

the hotel room was lovely
it was spacious and well-appointed
he liked the quietude because he really craved to rest

it had been a hectic day
he was dozing off when the music boomed
it probably emanated from the room directly opposite his

he was in for a rude awakening when the floor of his airy room quaked
his first impression was that the music was pounding away inside a person
how could he sleep when the music was continually screaming in ecstasy?

Isitshwala

she relished that traditional food
her children preferred rice and chicken
her meal usually consisted of a stiff
dumpling made from corn or grain
she ate that dough with okra or other vegies
the stiff dumpling was known as *isitshwala*

Mopani Worms

dried and salted

_____

a delicacy that saw an eater

swallow up his tongue

A Done Deal

the view could be blurred by
roaring and furious mists over
high mountains and sharp rocks
the road could be filled with thorns
and bottomless potholes and explosives
like an eagle—Thembani—soars beyond
the hurdles and prevailing situation around him
like an eagle he knows that as he soars the snakes
he is clutching in his fist are a done and defeated deal
like one Isaac he is prospering in the face of adversities!

Esigodini Hills

fabulous sight
landforms snake up and down
in extraordinary humps
of Nature's poise and pride,
breasts of land projecting
into charged saddles—
midwifed to gush out milk
of purity and tranquility;
the hills—though
small in size,
short in height—
lug and beam
a beauty that towers
the sky of my sensuousness;

their warmth appendages
the body with a nobility priceless,
like a cup of undiluted water,
they stand out undisturbed,
unchallenged by the ever-jerky
wheels of seasons and weather;
during gusty days their music
makes love to my ears with
a rare calmness—
I feel altogether like
abandoning my journey for them,
crowning them my beautiful infinity,
during sun-drenched days—
their seemingly little panorama,
drowns and dazzles my eyes into captivity;
an image of snug oases—
unparalleled greening of my soul,
they snuggle me all the way to the apex
of amity and stimulation…
they vacillate between ideal and real,

I relish to no end
their serrated depressions and passages
that feel me with a passion
beyond mere touch and tour,
they captivate my touch at will
I cannot give them a cursory look—
the harder I try to scuttle away
the further and so further
I gravitate into their cuddling glare;
they confer upon me the throne
of Nature's dutiful and indebted admirer
of the stupendous dexterity of our Creator;
the little hills that dominate my dreams—
those that epitomise a hustle-free haven
for the breezy incubation and birth
of a romance and a love of a lifetime;
those are my little hills that heal my soul,
they will define and refine my life
so that I get to appreciate the meaning
of dreams and days—
I am not surprised to hear that
these hills are lovers' haven,
the scenery is just compelling,
the shrubs and trees ooze a lively life;
the serenity is so delightful that
it promotes a refreshing union of hearts;
they are like alternative therapies—
the remedies of matters of the heart,
the birds` chirping –mellow
mends troubled souls—
melts bitterness and rancour—
nurses and mesmerises the ears
beyond any measurable fears!
the shrubs and trees beget an aroma
that makes a mockery of artificial perfumes,
those hills heal my soul in a high manner!

Romance Tourism

It could have been casual
Maybe it was a serious relationship
It delivered an education they both did not even grasp
They dealt with mannerisms and accents and food choices
They learnt to winnow idiosyncrasies from cultural practices

It was wild and wet like a raging river
There was something underlying and undying about it
It was the mystery of the culturally-embedded fire ravaging
Sometimes they strolled into the costal hotels and saw wonder of wonders
Locals and foreigners dancing to sizzling live music and tucking into premium meats

Rich older women in the young loving arms of poor local men who received gifts and cash
They seemed to enjoy succulent seafood and topped it off with beer and romantic carousing
The locals and foreigners` affairs were said to be boosting what people termed *romance tourism*

Voices In The Caves

I think …
of sites,
of rites,
of city,
of rusticity.

I think…
of spirituality,
of audacity,
of belief,
of misbelief .

I think…
of oldness,
of modernity,
of the unknown,
of the known.
.
I have heard of sacred sites
That people cannot
or should not tamper with
or they risk losing their mind.

I have heard chilling stories
of caves which swallow up those who
disrespectfully stray into their depths.

I have heard of consecrated sites
where shoes are put away when doing rites,
where custodians of the places rule supreme.

Hills that are a reflection of natural beauty
These little peaks talk of a presence of spirituality,
Someone finds oneself talking with reverence,
Someone finds oneself walking with elegance,

Remembering the myths and legends of other hills.

l was told of the myths and mysteries of Shamba hills,
of inexplicable voices and shadowy presences,
of bizarre fires and uncanny happenings.

For those who lived in the city and its ignorant audacity,
elders emphasised   respect for those sites,
for each place has its own rites.

I was told how those who desecrated against such sites
found stupidity in their wisdom and audacity
when outlandish things
dogged them.

Hailing from Bulawayo in Zimbabwe, Ndaba Sibanda is a poet, novelist, and nonfiction writer who has a passion for themes and topics around conservation, nature, development and justice. A three-time Pushcart, National Arts Merit Awards, Mary Ballard Poetry Chapbook Prize and the Best of the Net Prose nominee, Sibanda`s book *Notes, Themes, Things And Other Things: Confronting Controversies, Contradictions And Indoctrinations was* considered for *The 2019 Restless Book Prize for New Immigrant Writing in Nonfiction.* Ndaba`s novel *Cabinet Meetings: Of Big And Small Preys* was considered for *The Graywolf Press Africa Prize 2018.* His five titles are on the Barnes and Noble list of 2024 Best books.